The First
Moon Landing

Dale Anderson

WORLD ALMANAC® LIBRARY

Please visit our web site at: www.worldalmanaclibrary.com
For a free color catalog describing World Almanac® Library's list of high-quality
books and multimedia programs, call 1-800-848-2928 (USA) or 1-800-387-3178
(Canada). World Almanac® Library's fax: (414) 332-3567.

Library of Congress Cataloging-in-Publication Data

Anderson, Dale, 1953-
    The first moon landing / by Dale Anderson.
      p. cm. — (Landmark events in American history)
    Summary: Describes the background, planning, accomplishment, and aftermath
of Apollo 11, the first manned mission to land on the moon.
    Includes bibliographical references and index.
    ISBN 0-8368-5378-4 (lib. bdg.)
    ISBN 0-8368-5406-3 (softcover)
    1. Project Apollo (U.S.)—Juvenile literature. 2. Apollo 11 (Spacecraft)—Juvenile
literature. 3. Space flight to the moon—Juvenile literature. [1. Project Apollo (U.S.).
2. Apollo 11 (Spacecraft). 3. Space flight to the moon.] I. Title. II. Series.
    TL789.8.U6A5115   2003
    629.45'4'0973—dc21   2003047913

First published in 2004 by
World Almanac® Library
330 West Olive Street, Suite 100
Milwaukee, WI 53212 USA

Copyright © 2004 by World Almanac® Library.

Produced by Discovery Books
Editor: Sabrina Crewe
Designer and page production: Sabine Beaupré
Photo researcher: Sabrina Crewe
Maps and diagrams: Stefan Chabluk
World Almanac® Library editorial direction: Mark J. Sachner
World Almanac® Library art direction: Tammy Gruenewald
World Almanac® Library production: Beth Meinholz and Jessica Yanke

Photo credits: Corbis: cover, pp. 5, 6, 7, 12, 17, 19, 21, 23, 24, 30, 37, 39 (bottom);
NASA: pp. 4, 8, 9, 10, 11, 13, 14, 15, 16 (both), 18, 20, 22, 25, 26, 27, 28 (both),
31, 32, 33, 34, 35, 36, 38, 39 (top), 40, 42, 43; NASA/ACS Science Team: p. 41;
The New York Times Co./Library of Congress: p. 29.

Printed in the United States of America

1 2 3 4 5 6 7 8 9 07 06 05 04 03

Contents

Introduction

The footprints left on the Moon by Armstrong and Aldrin are still there. There is no **atmosphere** on the Moon and therefore no wind to disturb the footprints.

A Giant Leap

At 10:56 P.M. Eastern Daylight Time on July 20, 1969, a foot enclosed in a bulky boot settled into some powdery dirt. As the foot came down, its owner proclaimed, "That's one small step for man, one giant leap for mankind."

The speaker was astronaut Neil Armstrong, and his step made him the first person to set foot on the Moon. For the first time in history, a human was touching the surface of a body in space other than Earth. It was probably the most-watched step ever, with about 500 million people around the world viewing television images of this historic **lunar** landing.

Armstrong and two other astronauts were on the U.S. space mission called *Apollo 11*—the first manned mission to land on the Moon. Although their journey lasted only a few days, it marked the fulfillment of a long-held human dream and the realization of a president's goal.

The President's Challenge

By the early 1960s, scientists and engineers in the **Soviet Union** had enjoyed two major successes in space. They had put the first **satellite** into space and put the first human into **orbit** around Earth.

This was during the Cold War, when the United States and the Soviet Union were locked in a bitter struggle to gain influence around the world. The Soviet success in space embarrassed many U.S. leaders. They felt that the United States needed to regain its status as leader of the free world. The nation needed to achieve something dramatic to show that the U.S. space program could beat the Soviet one. And so a U.S. president, John F. Kennedy, challenged Americans to put a human on the Moon before the end of the 1960s.

Dreaming of the Moon

Since the nineteenth century, scientists had sought ways to send vehicles into space. While there was much talk about Mars and life on other planets, the Moon was the focus of many scientists' thoughts. After all, the Moon is the nearest body to Earth in the Universe—about 240,000 miles (385,000 kilometers) away—and the one most visible at night. Interest in travel to the Moon grew more intense after French writer Jules Verne published two exciting and popular science fiction novels: *From the Earth to the Moon* in 1865 and *Around the Moon* in 1870. Verne's novels captured the imaginations of ordinary people and helped inspire important space scientists of the early 1900s.

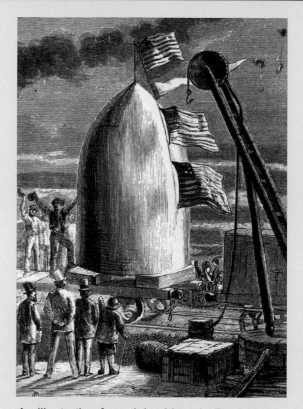

An illustration from Jules Verne's *From the Earth to the Moon*.

Chapter 1

The Space Race

Competition in Space

On October 4, 1957, the Soviet Union shocked the world by launching the satellite *Sputnik* into orbit. The next month, the Soviets scored another triumph by sending a dog into space in *Sputnik 2*. Although the dog died when the spacecraft ran out of oxygen, the Soviets had shown that a living being could survive in space.

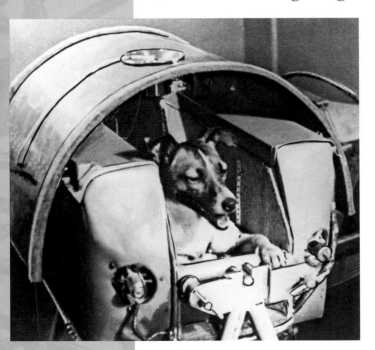

Meanwhile, the United States tried launching a satellite, but the rocket exploded. Not until 1958 did the United States succeed in sending a satellite, *Explorer*, into orbit.

The space race had begun. The Soviet Union and the United States began competing in earnest, sending up many satellites. In preparation for putting humans in space, the Soviets sent up more dogs and the Americans sent monkeys, mice, and chimps. In September 1959, the Soviets beat the Americans once more, when *Luna 2* became the first unmanned **probe** to land on the Moon.

Soviet space dog Laika nestles inside *Sputnik 2* for her journey into space in 1957. The trip was the first proof that living creatures could survive outside Earth's atmosphere.

The First Man in Space

On April 12, 1961, the Soviets put the first person in orbit around Earth. **Cosmonaut** Yuri Gagarin completed one orbit, sending back radio messages about what he felt and saw and about how the spacecraft performed. Gagarin's 108-minute flight made him the world's first space hero.

Over the next twenty-six months, the Soviets launched five more one-person flights. On one flight, lasting almost five days, they made eighty-one orbits. They put two craft in orbit at the same time. They also put the first woman, Valentina Tereshkova, into space in 1963.

A Soviet postcard celebrates Yuri Gagarin's achievements as the first person in space. Gagarin later served as a roving ambassador for the Soviet Union. He died in 1968 while training for a return to space.

The Cold War

During the 1950s and 1960s, the United States was caught in a conflict with the Soviet Union. The two countries had joined together during World War II to fight Nazi Germany. After the war, however, deep differences divided them. In the United States, society was based on the idea of individual freedom. In a system known as capitalism, business owners could operate as they chose. In the Soviet Union, under communism, society was based on the idea of common good. The government owned and controlled all businesses.

The two huge powers struggled against each other around the world. Each one tried to convert countries to its own political system. They never fought each other directly, although both sent troops to fight against allies of the other. One reason that the two nations never fought directly was that both had large supplies of nuclear weapons. With these bombs, and the missiles to deliver them, they could easily destroy each other.

This rivalry made the space race important to both sides, and not just because success in space would make them look better than the other side. The new **technology** of space could also be applied to making more powerful weapons.

On May 5, 1961, the United States launched its first manned space-flight from Cape Canaveral, Florida. The spacecraft reached an altitude of 116.5 miles (187.5 km).

Americans in Space

While the Soviets enjoyed their successes, the United States moved ahead—slowly —with its own one-person space program. It included six flights that were all part of Project Mercury. The National Aeronautics and Space Administration (NASA), an agency of the national government, ran the program.

The first American in space was Alan Shepard. His flight on May 5, 1961, lasted only fifteen minutes. Unlike Yuri Gagarin, he did not orbit Earth. His craft simply followed an arc-shaped path into space and back down.

Two and a half months later, Gus Grissom took a similar flight. Everything went smoothly until Grissom's spacecraft finished its mission and splashed down in the Atlantic Ocean. As he was completing some final checks, the hatch suddenly blew open. The capsule began to fill with water, and Grissom had to escape quickly. He was saved by a rescue team, but the capsule sank to the bottom of the ocean. It looked like yet another failure for the U.S. space program.

In early 1962—nearly a year after Gagarin's flight—John Glenn became the first American to orbit Earth. During his flight of almost five hours, Glenn chatted about his reactions to the changes in gravity, the four sunsets he witnessed, and the oceans and land masses he saw down below. He was acclaimed as a hero, and about four million people attended a tickertape parade in his honor in New York City.

Kennedy's Pledge

The last three Mercury flights, in 1962 and 1963, tested engineering, procedure, and increased flight time. Americans, however, were looking ahead to bigger and better things. Shortly after Shepard's flight, President Kennedy had given NASA a bold new mission. In 1961, he spoke to Congress about his goals in the Cold

President John F. Kennedy speaks to Congress in May 1961 about the goals of the U.S. space program. He did not live to see the realization of his commitment, made that day, to land a human on the Moon before the end of the decade.

A Bold Goal

"I believe that this nation should commit itself to achieving the goal, before this decade is out, of landing a man on the Moon and returning him safely to Earth. No single project in this period will be more impressive to mankind or more important for the long-range exploration of space."

President John F. Kennedy, speech to Congress, May 25, 1961

War. In that speech, the president gave the space race a clear focus: to put a person on the Moon.

Possible Strategies

NASA planners decided they would need more than one spacecraft for a Moon mission. This meant that the astronauts would have to **rendezvous** two vehicles, or steer them to be near each other. They would also have to carry out **docking**, or joining the two spacecraft together. So NASA now had to design, build, and test these spacecraft. It also had to test the **navigation** techniques astronauts could use to plot their course through space. In addition, astronauts would need steering techniques to carry out rendezvous and docking while traveling at 18,000 miles (29,000 km) per hour!

NASA had to address one more important issue before it could carry out a Moon mission. Could human beings, or even machines, survive in space for the ten days—or more—that it took to get to the Moon and back?

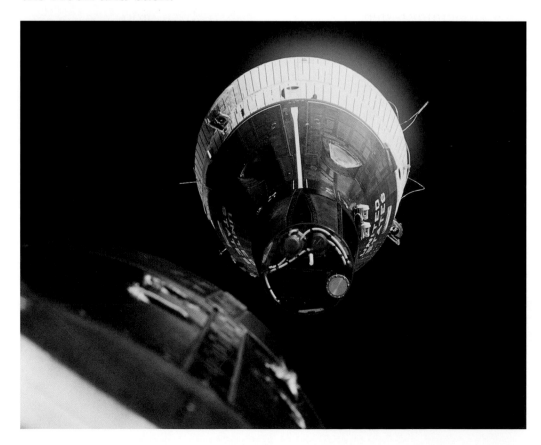

This photo of *Gemini 7* was taken from *Gemini 6* as the two spacecraft made the first space rendezvous on December 15, 1965.

In June 1965, Edward White, seen here, climbed out of *Gemini 4* to float in space, secured to the spacecraft by two cords. Aleksey Leonov of the Soviet Union had become the first person to "walk" in space a few months earlier.

Project Gemini

Project Gemini tested NASA's solutions to these problems. Ten Gemini flights carried two men each. Unlike the first two missions, *Gemini 3* astronauts were the first to control the spacecraft using an on-board computer.

Gemini 4 produced the spectacular image of Edward White "walking" in space in 1965, the first American to do so. Two long cords kept White attached to his spacecraft while he used a handheld gas gun to control his direction. Returning to the spacecraft after his spacewalk, White said, "was the saddest moment in my life."

In December 1965, *Gemini 6* achieved the first rendezvous of two spacecraft, when it flew within one foot (0.3 meter) of *Gemini 7*. With a fourteen-day voyage, *Gemini 7* also proved that people could indeed survive in space long enough to go to the Moon and back. *Gemini 8* was the first mission to test docking procedures, when pilot Neil Armstrong joined the space capsule to another vehicle already in orbit. Four later flights in 1966 perfected other techniques.

Free in Space

"It's not like floating in water. In water you feel support, the slipping through the medium. In space you don't have that sensation."

Aleksey Leonov, describing his Voskhod 2 spacewalk, 1965

"This is the greatest experience; it's just tremendous . . . . Right now, I'm standing on my head and I'm looking right down and looks like we're coming up on the coast of California."

Edward White, describing his Gemini 4 spacewalk, 1965

Chapter 2

The Apollo Program

Apollo Spacecraft

After Gemini, the next step in the race to the Moon was the Apollo program. Engineers used the program to solve several problems.

First, they needed a spacecraft that could go to the Moon, land on it, take off from it, and return. Engineers designed a spacecraft with three modules, or pieces, that worked together. The **command module (CM)** made the long trips between Earth and the Moon. It held the astronauts' living space and the instruments used to control the craft. The **lunar module (LM)** made the shorter trip from the CM to the Moon's surface and back. The lunar module would have two parts: a descent stage to land on the Moon; and an ascent stage, powered by rockets, to take the astronauts back into space to rejoin the CM. The **service module** contained equipment, supplies, and the rocket that would send the CM back to Earth.

A Powerful Rocket

Second, engineers needed a rocket powerful enough to push the spacecraft to the Moon. The answer was the huge Saturn V rocket, 36 stories tall and weighing 5.8 million pounds (2.6 million kilograms). This powerful rocket had three stages, or sections. The first two stages launched the spacecraft out of the atmosphere and into orbit around Earth. The third stage sent the spacecraft to the Moon.

During a press conference at the start of the Apollo program, models of the three modules were unveiled for the Moon mission. On the left is the command module. In the middle is the lunar module with its descent stage at the bottom and ascent stage on top. The large service module stands on the right.

New Technology

The 1950s and 1960s, when the space program began, were a time of many advances in technology. Television became a part of society, although most people still had black-and-white sets. Many conveniences that we now take for granted in the home, factories, and other businesses were still under development. These large computers could not do what the smallest computer can do today.

In 1958, the scientists who sent the first U.S. satellite into space used a **slide rule** to make calculations because there were no electronic calculators. That same year, however, an important invention, the silicone chip, took place and soon changed technology and human capabilities in countless ways. The silicon chip can contain millions of the electrical circuits needed to process information and control all kinds of devices, especially computers. This invention made the Moon landing possible—*Apollo 11* was guided by a computer with five thousand silicon chips. Technology advanced rapidly in the following years. In 1975, an astronaut on an Apollo mission carried a pocket calculator with more power than the computer on board *Apollo 11*.

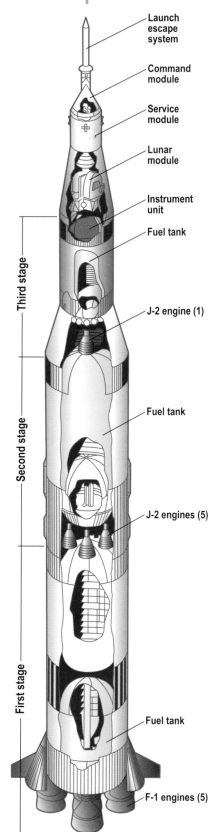

Launch escape system

Command module

Service module

Lunar module

Instrument unit

Fuel tank

Third stage

J-2 engine (1)

Fuel tank

Second stage

J-2 engines (5)

First stage

Fuel tank

F-1 engines (5)

This diagram (right) shows a cutaway of the Saturn V rocket that launched *Apollo 11* (above). The command and service modules are just small parts at the top of the huge rocket. The lunar module is inside, just below the service module.

Buzz Aldrin descends from the lunar module in a space suit that protects him from an environment without an atmosphere. His helmet has a gold-plated visor that keeps out the Sun's unfiltered rays. On his back is an oxygen supply.

Dedicated Workers

"I've been with Grumman for forty-two years. I've worked on every major program. I never worked on a program that was so all-encompassing, that required total, total concentration constantly for such a long period of time. . . . The LM—that thing went into years of exhausting days."

Bill Voorhest, manager at Northrop Grumman, makers of the lunar module

Problems and Solutions

The Apollo series of missions each had three astronauts. To survive on the Moon, the astronauts needed special space suits. Engineers designed suits to keep the astronauts' bodies at a comfortable temperature and air pressure. The suits also gave them the oxygen they needed to breathe. The helmets allowed astronauts to see while keeping out harmful light rays.

The biggest problem that NASA faced was how to navigate the spacecraft to the Moon and back. This meant precisely calculating the position of Earth, the Moon, and the spacecraft at all times while all three were moving and being affected by one another's gravity. The mathematical equations involved were so long and complex that many scientists felt they were impossible to solve. The solution was provided by the new science of computers. These new machines could make the calculations that overwhelmed people.

Controlling the Flight

A key part of the Apollo program was Mission Control. Workers at the Kennedy Space Center in Florida controlled operations until launch. Then people at the Manned Spacecraft Center in Houston, Texas, took over. This was Mission Control, a busy station where scientists and engineers kept track of all the different systems

The hub of Mission Control was one large room filled with desktop monitors and larger screens on the wall. During Apollo missions, it was manned by four teams of flight controllers working shifts around the clock.

on board the spacecraft, such as the engines, guidance, and life support. Doctors checked the astronauts' temperature, heart rate, and other vital signs by reading results relayed back from the spacecraft. Top managers gathered all the information they received and advised the astronauts on how to navigate, conduct experiments, or solve problems. They even reminded the crew when to rest.

The capsule communicator, or "capcom," was the link person between Mission Control and the astronauts in flight. The capcom

Women of the Apollo Program

Only a few women worked in the Apollo space program, but some played vital roles. Peggy Hewitt headed a team of forty engineers responsible for the lunar module. Like many others in the program, she had started out building military airplanes during World War II. Eilene Galloway worked at the Library of Congress and served as an advisor to several Senate committees on space.

Myrtice Holland carried out **soldering** on the LM. But hiring her was no simple matter. State law in New York—where the LM was built—banned women from working overtime. Long hours and weekend work, however, were often necessary for people working in the space program. Since Holland was one of the very few solderers that NASA approved for this important work, the state law had to be changed.

was always another astronaut, a person who could understand the **perspective** of the astronauts in space.

Disaster

The Apollo program began with a disaster. On January 27, 1967, astronauts Gus Grissom, Edward White, and Roger Chaffee entered the command module of their *Apollo 1* spacecraft. The capsule was sitting on top of a rocket on the Florida launching pad. The crew was testing systems in preparation for a launch the following month. In the midst of these tests, a short circuit in the wiring started a fire, which spread instantly in the craft's pure oxygen atmosphere. The astronauts tried to escape but did not have enough time to open the hatch. Grissom, White, and Chaffee all died.

Above is the command module of *Apollo 1*, in which three astronauts died when they were trapped by a sudden fire. The astronauts who died were (left to right) Edward White, Gus Grissom, and Roger Chaffee.

Risks of the Unknown

The *Apollo 1* disaster highlighted the experimental nature of the space program. Everything being designed for space travel was new and very complex. For example, the outside of the lunar vehicle had so many rivets holding pieces together that if only 5 percent of them were incorrectly joined, about two thousand different things could go wrong as a result.

The astronauts knew the risks they ran. Grissom himself had written, "We flew with the knowledge that if something really went wrong up there, there wasn't the slightest hope of rescue." The astronauts tried to minimize those risks: Grissom had insisted that the tests on that fateful January day include a check of the emergency escape system. Sadly, the system had not yet been tested when the fire broke out.

Testing for Safety

After the *Apollo 1* fire, the Apollo program was halted while an investigation was carried out. NASA redesigned Apollo, adding extensive fire safety features and a hatch that could be quickly opened. Before sending astronauts back into space, however, NASA carried out several unmanned launches between late 1967 and early 1968. These missions tested the safety and reliability of the CM, LM, service module, and rocket; and as problems arose, engineers solved them.

Dress Rehearsals

Next, four Apollo missions put astronauts back in space. People on Earth were able to catch a glimpse of astronaut life through many television transmissions.

Coming Home
"I think I must have the feeling that the travelers in the old sailing ships used to have, going on a long voyage away from home. And now that we're headed back, I have that feeling of being proud of the trip, but still happy to be going home. . . . We'll see you back on that good Earth very soon."

William Anders of
Apollo 8, *1968*

This is the Kennedy Space Center in Florida, where all the Apollo missions began. The launch directors, center, are awaiting the liftoff of *Apollo 7*, the first manned spaceflight since the *Apollo 1* disaster.

Astronauts head out to a van that will carry them to their spaceship during the count-down for *Apollo 8*. It would become the first manned mission to orbit the Moon.

Apollo 7 tested the command module and service modules, as the astronauts used the newly designed controls to maneuver the craft. They also fired the rocket in the service module that would push the spacecraft back to Earth.

Apollo 8 was the first mission to reach the Moon, orbit it, and return to Earth. This mission tested the navigational calculations for

Early Manned Apollo Missions

Flight Number/Astronauts	Dates	Key Facts
7: Walter Schirra; Donn Eisele; R. Walter Cunningham	October 11–22, 1968	163 Earth orbits; tested command and service modules.
8: Frank Borman; James Lovell, Jr.; William Anders	December 21–27, 1968	First mission to reach and orbit Moon.
9: James McDivitt; David Scott; Russell Schweickart	March 3–13, 1969	Earth orbit; tested rocket and CM's and LM's ability to detach and dock.
10: Thomas Stafford; John Young; Eugene Cernan	May 18–26, 1969	Traveled to Moon and back; LM descended close to Moon's surface.
11: Neil Armstrong; Buzz Aldrin; Michael Collins	July 16–24, 1969	First mission to land on Moon.

flying to the Moon. It also verified that the service module rocket could power the craft back to Earth. During this trip, the astronauts were far enough away from Earth to see the whole planet. James Lovell described the planet as "about as big as the end of my thumb."

Apollo 9 tested the lunar module in Earth orbit. James McDivitt, David Scott, and Russell Schweickart separated the CM and service module, turned the CM around, and docked with the LM. Schweickart and Scott took a spacewalk in the new lunar space suits. Then McDivitt and Schweickart separated the LM, flew it separately for some time, cast off the descent stage, and docked once again with the CM.

NASA now knew that all the equipment worked as planned. But before risking a landing on the Moon, all the maneuvers had to be tested one more time, around the Moon itself, because the pull of gravity there was different than around Earth. In May 1969, *Apollo 10* carried out those tests.

It was on *Apollo 10* that everything was tested for the actual Moon landing. This is a view of the *Apollo 10* command module above the Moon's surface, taken from the lunar module after it separated from the command module.

Apollo 11

Choosing the Crew

When NASA chose Neil Armstrong, Buzz Aldrin, and Michael Collins as the crew for *Apollo 11*, the three astronauts did not know that they would become the first people to reach the Moon. All the crews were chosen long before their eventual flight date—they needed time to train. No one knew, however, which Apollo mission would be the first to land on the Moon. That depended on how many flights were needed to check out the equipment and

The Astronauts

All the *Apollo 11* astronauts were born in 1930. **Edwin Eugene (Buzz) Aldrin** was the first scientist astronaut. He attended the U.S. Military Academy at West Point and served as a fighter pilot during the Korean War. At NASA, before *Apollo 11*, Aldrin made significant contributions to the development of the procedures and computer systems used by Gemini and Apollo. After *Apollo 11*, he ran the air force test pilot school and worked in high-tech businesses.

Neil Armstrong (left), Michael Collins (center), and Buzz Aldrin (right).

On a scholarship from the U.S. Navy, **Neil Alden Armstrong** studied aeronautical engineering. He then served in Korea as a pilot. Afterward, Armstrong became a civilian test pilot. He has been described by colleagues as "probably the best jet test pilot in the world." *Apollo 11* was his last spaceflight, and he later taught engineering at an Ohio university.

Michael Collins also went to West Point. He served in the air force as a fighter pilot in Europe and later became a test pilot. Collins took part in both the Gemini and Apollo programs. He retired after *Apollo 11*, and for many years, he was director of the National Air and Space Museum.

systems. All of the Apollo astronauts were expected to be mentally, physically, and technically prepared to serve on any mission. But it was the crew of *Apollo 11* that got the job.

Neil Armstrong commanded the mission. He was also the pilot of the lunar module, called the *Eagle*. Buzz Aldrin would fly in the LM with Armstrong, monitoring its systems and advising him as he flew. Michael Collins was the pilot of the command module, *Columbia*. If anything went wrong with the LM, he would attempt to save Armstrong and Aldrin.

Liftoff!

On the morning of July 16, 1969, about eight thousand special guests and two thousand journalists filled the viewing stands near the Kennedy Space Center. Nearly one million people lined the Florida beaches, and hundreds of millions around the world watched on television as the Saturn V rocket began to roar, carrying *Apollo 11* into the sky.

In under three minutes, the rocket was more than 40 miles (64 km) up and traveling at more than 5,000 miles (8,000 km) per hour. At this point, the first stage was

About one million people watched from the beaches of Cape Kennedy as *Apollo 11* was launched. Cape Kennedy was previously—and is now once more —named Cape Canaveral.

A Rough Ride

"It was, I thought, quite a rough ride in the first fifteen seconds or so. . . . I don't mean that the engines were rough, and I don't mean that it was noisy. But it was very busy—that's the best word. It was steering like crazy. . . . But the jerkiness quieted down after about fifteen seconds."

Michael Collins, describing the liftoff of Apollo 11

out of fuel, and that part of the rocket was dropped off.

The second stage rockets kicked in, pushing the spacecraft even higher and faster. Just twelve minutes after the launch, the astronauts were speeding along at 17,400 miles (28,000 km) per hour and had begun to orbit Earth. Less than three hours after takeoff, *Apollo 11* left Earth's orbit and turned toward the Moon. *Apollo 11* was on its way.

To the Moon

Inside the command module, as else-where in space, the astronauts experienced the weightlessness that comes when people get away from Earth's gravitational pull. They floated around the cabin and had to strap or wedge themselves in if they wanted to stay put. While cruising to the Moon, which took three days, the crew did their chores in the command module *Columbia*. They chlorinated the drinking water, charged batteries, and dumped waste water. They made some course corrections needed to keep themselves on track.

The three astronauts had public relations work to do, too. NASA knew that millions around the world were following the flight. Armstrong, Aldrin, and Collins hosted several television broadcasts showing people what life was like in space.

While the spacecraft flew, it rotated constantly so that one side would not be damaged by the heat of the Sun, which was more intense than on Earth because of the lack of atmosphere. When they got closer to the Moon, its shape blocked out the Sun. Collins explained, "Now we're able to see stars again and recognize constellations for the first time on the trip. The sky's full of stars." He

Within minutes of the launch, at an altitude of about 40 miles (64 km), the first stage of the Saturn V rocket was used up. This picture shows the Saturn V second and third stages pulling away from the first stage.

also described the "earth-shine"—the light from Earth, which streamed through the spacecraft's windows. Collins said that the light was "so bright you can read a book by it."

Getting Ready

Apollo 11 started to orbit the Moon on July 19. Armstrong and Aldrin then began checking the

This is Neil Armstrong in the cockpit of *Columbia* on his way to the Moon. The three astronauts stayed in the CM until it was time for Armstrong and Aldrin to enter the lunar module and make their descent.

Everyday Life in Space

Living in space presented some challenges. The astronauts on *Apollo 11* had about seventy freeze-dried meals to choose from, including spaghetti and chicken stew. They also had sliced bread and sandwich spreads, cold drinks and coffee, and snacks such as dried peaches.

During their rest periods in the command module, Collins, the command pilot, slept strapped into one of the reclining seats so that he would not accidentally hit any switches. He wore a small headset in case Mission Control had to contact him in an emergency. Armstrong and Aldrin used sleeping bags under the seats.

Since there was no bathroom in the capsule, the astronauts used special plastic bags for their urine and bowel movements. Although they could shave, they could not wash and so used wipes and tissues instead. All three were very ready for a shower when they returned to Earth.

The crew found their weightlessness enjoyable. When Aldrin sent transmissions to Earth, he told audiences, "I've been having a ball floating around inside here." He later added, "After a while . . . you sort of get tired of rattling around . . . so you tend to find a little corner somewhere . . . to wedge yourself in."

systems on the lunar module. Mission Control would not give the go-ahead for the *Eagle* to land without making sure that systems such as life support, guidance, propulsion, and radar were working.

Finally, clearance came from Mission Control. During the twelfth orbit, the command module and lunar module separated. When the modules came to the Earth side of the Moon and communication was again possible with Earth, Armstrong told NASA, "The *Eagle* has wings," meaning the LM was now on its own.

Descent

After separation, the *Eagle* and *Columbia* flew close to each other so that Collins could check the outside of the LM for any damage. Then the two modules parted. *Columbia,* with Collins on board, continued to orbit the Moon. On July 20, the *Eagle* began its descent toward an area of the Moon called the Sea of Tranquility.

Computers controlled the descent. But at about 30,000 feet (9,000 meters) above the surface, alarms began to sound—the computers had too much information to process. Armstrong and Aldrin had to spend a few moments handling the situation and could not keep their eyes on the descent. When Armstrong looked

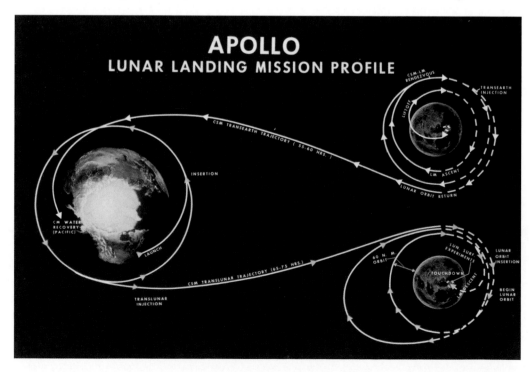

This diagram shows the plan for the Moon landing mission. The lower track follows the flight from Earth and descent to the Moon; the upper track shows the return journey to Earth.

A photograph from the command module *Columbia* shows the exciting moment when the lunar module, the *Eagle* (left), parted from *Columbia* in orbit around the Moon. Dangling from the bottom of the *Eagle*'s landing pods are **sensors** to help with landing on the Moon's surface.

out again, he saw they were about 1,000 feet (300 m) from the ground and heading for a crater filled with huge rocks. He took manual control and moved the LM away from the area. With only 5 percent of the descent fuel and ninety seconds of time left, he began looking for a place to land. The lower they got, the more dust the LM's engine kicked up from the Moon's surface, making it harder to see the ground.

Landing on the Moon

At last, with only seven seconds of fuel left, the LM made a soft landing. A few moments later, Neil Armstrong said his first famous words on the Moon, "Houston, Tranquility Base here. The *Eagle* has landed." Charley Duke, the capcom that day, revealed the tension felt at Mission Control with his reply: "You've got a bunch of guys [down here] about to turn blue. We're breathing again."

One Small Step

Armstrong and Aldrin were supposed to get some sleep before they left the *Eagle*, but they were too excited. A few hours after landing,

Neil Armstrong holds the pole bearing a U.S. flag as Buzz Aldrin adjusts the mounting. The flag had a rod running through its top to hold it up because of the lack of wind on the Moon.

Famous Words

Armstrong's first words as he stepped onto the Moon's surface have become famous. But they were not exactly what he meant to say. The speech he had planned and rehearsed was, "That's one small step for a man; one giant leap for mankind." But the excitement of the moment was apparently too much for the usually cool astronaut, and he left out the word "a."

Armstrong did not realize what he had actually said until well after the crew returned to Earth. When he heard about it, he commented ruefully, "I really did it. I blew the first words on the Moon, didn't I?"

after many checks and preparations, the astronauts came out of the LM. A camera on the outside of the craft sent pictures of Armstrong climbing down the ladder and stepping onto the lunar surface. Aldrin, who followed, described the moonscape as "magnificent desolation."

Armstrong and Aldrin's moonwalk lasted about two hours. Getting around on the Moon was no easy matter because of the reduced gravity there. The astronauts had to lean forward in the direction they wanted to go and then take a few steps to build up speed. To stop, they had to slow down ahead of time or else overshoot their destination.

Getting to Work
In spite of the difficulties, Armstrong and Aldrin got a great

deal of work done on the Moon. They collected rocks for analysis on Earth and set up various scientific experiments. They also installed a better television camera than the one that had shown Armstrong coming down the ladder. New, clearer images were then sent back to Earth and seen on television by millions.

Finally, the two astronauts left some mementos. They planted a U.S. flag on the Moon's surface. Then they put up a plaque that reads, "Here men from the planet Earth first set foot upon the Moon, July 1969, A.D. We came in peace for all mankind." They also left tributes honoring Russian and American astronauts who had died while in the space program.

The steel plaque commemorating the *Apollo 11* landing was bolted onto the landing gear of the lunar module. The descent stage of the LM, with the plaque attached, remains on the Moon today.

The Big Test

Liftoff from the Moon was a tense time for Mission Control. It was the first time anyone had tried to launch a rocket from a place other than Earth. And that first try was coming with two men on board. Aboard the CM, Collins worried that something might go wrong, and he would not be able to rescue his fellow astronauts. But the rockets fired and the ascent stage of the LM separated from the descent stage just as planned. Armstrong and Aldrin steered the *Eagle* into orbit around the Moon and caught up with *Columbia*.

Coming Home

Once the two craft were docked, the LM astronauts reboarded *Columbia*, and the crew jettisoned the *Eagle*. They fired the engine that would take them out of lunar orbit and send them home. *Apollo 11* finished its eight-day journey by splashing down in the Pacific Ocean on July 24, 1969.

As soon as they emerged from *Columbia*, Armstrong, Aldrin, and Collins were placed in biological isolation suits. Scientists did not know if the Moon had any living organisms. Some worried that the astronauts could bring back microscopic life-forms dangerous to plants, animals, or humans on Earth. The three astronauts were

The *Apollo 11* astronauts share a joke with President Richard Nixon from inside their quarantine trailer.

28

flown to an area at the Manned Spacecraft Center in Houston. The astronauts had to stay in **quarantine** in a trailer for more than two weeks.

A Big Welcome

The astronauts of *Apollo 11* were hailed as great heroes around the world. In the United States, Armstrong, Aldrin, and Collins had a tickertape parade in New York, a reception in Chicago attended by fifteen thousand people, and a state dinner with President Richard Nixon, among many other events. Then they went on a whirlwind tour of six continents.

Skeptics and Believers

Some people did not believe that humans had reached the Moon. They thought it was a trick of television or maybe a piece of propaganda put out by the U.S. government. But the imagination of many others was fired by the journey. Ninety thousand people wrote to Pan American World Airways for reservations on the first commercial flight to the Moon, which they were promoting to happen in the year 2000—it didn't happen.

The entire front page of *The New York Times* on July 21, 1969, was devoted to the Moon landing. In spite of television and newspaper coverage, some people thought the whole thing was a hoax.

Remembering the Day

"I couldn't believe it! I actually walked outside and looked at the Moon. I just stood there in amazement, staring up at the real Moon—not the one on TV. I just stared and thought about how there was somebody actually up there walking on that dot in the sky."

Jack French, sculptor, remembering thirty years later what it was like to see the Moon landing, 1999

Exploring the Moon

Apollo 12

NASA sent six more missions to the Moon after *Apollo 11*. The first of them, *Apollo 12*, left Earth on November 14, 1969. Astronauts Pete Conrad and Alan Bean settled the LM down only 600 feet (180 m) from *Surveyor 3*, a NASA probe that had landed on the Moon more than two years before. They collected rocks and soil and took photographs.

The Sun shines in a dark sky over the lunar module of *Apollo 14*. Even during the Moon's "day," when the Sun is visible, the sky is still dark because there is no atmosphere around the Moon to scatter the Sun's rays and make the sky light.

Later Manned Apollo Missions

Flight Number/Astronauts	Dates	Key Facts
12: Charles (Pete) Conrad; Richard Gordon; Alan Bean	November 14–24, 1969	Spent more than a day on Moon's surface doing experiments.
13: James Lovell, Jr.; John Swigert; Fred Haise	April 11–17, 1970	Never landed on Moon due to damage to spacecraft; safely returned to Earth.
14: Alan Shepard; Stuart Roosa; Edgar Mitchell	January 31– February 9, 1971	Did experiments to learn about Moon's interior; last crew to be quarantined.
15: David Scott; Alfred Worden; James Irwin	June 26–July 7, 1971	First use of vehicle that could move over Moon's surface; improved space suits.
16: John Young; Thomas Mattingly; Charles Duke	April 16–27, 1972	Set up astronomical observatory on Moon's surface.
17: Eugene Cernan; Ronald Evans; Harrison Schmitt	December 7–19, 1972	Longest stay on Moon's surface (75 hours).

Apollo 13

Halfway to the Moon on *Apollo 13*, an oxygen tank exploded and another tank began leaking. The oxygen was needed to make electricity for the engines, to produce water, and for breathing. The crew was in grave danger. To save as much power as possible, the astronauts had to shut down the CM. For the next four days, the three astronauts crowded into the LM while engineers on the ground frantically worked to get the crew home.

The astronauts had enough oxygen to breathe, but electricity and water were in short supply. They saved water by rationing it and saved power by turning off lights and letting the temperature drop to near freezing as *Apollo 13* limped back to Earth. When they got closer,

The Drive to Explore
"Nothing will stop us. The road to the stars is steep and dangerous. But we're not afraid. . . . Space flights can't be stopped. This isn't the work of any one man or even a group of men. It is a historical process which mankind is carrying out in accordance with the natural laws of human development."

Soviet cosmonaut Yuri Gagarin, 1967

David Scott, *Apollo 15* commander, has set up all kinds of experiments on the Moon. Around him are bores and drills for exploring beneath the Moon's surface. In the center foreground is a wind experiment.

Discoveries on the Moon

Apollo astronauts brought back rocks older than any found on Earth—one was nicknamed the "Genesis rock" because it was so ancient. Some rocks brought back from the Moon contained minerals never before seen. One was named "armalcolite" after the three *Apollo 11* astronauts ("arm" for Armstrong, "al" for Aldrin, "col" for Collins, and "ite" because it is a mineral). This mineral came from meteorites—rocks that move through space—that had hit the Moon's surface. Later, it was found in craters left by meteorites that had hit Earth.

The Moon is very ancient, and its early history reveals information about the formation of Earth, Mars, Venus, and Mercury, including that the Moon and Earth had similar origins and were made of similar materials. Volcanoes had erupted on the Moon, as they have on Earth. Many meteorites have slammed into the Moon's surface. Earth has evidence of this kind of activity also.

Because the Moon has no atmosphere, there is no air and no temperature control—it is baking hot in the heat of the Sun and gets freezing cold at night. There are no living creatures, nor evidence that anything ever lived there. In 1998, however, hydrogen was detected at the Moon's poles, which means that there may be water—and therefore potential for life—in the form of millions of tons of ice frozen in the Moon's surface layer. Plans for a space station on the Moon have been discussed at NASA, and the presence of water would mean the possibility of growing food.

Apollo 17 astronaut Harrison Schmitt stands by a huge split boulder on the Moon's surface.

the crew powered up the CM, which they needed in order to enter Earth's atmosphere. They dropped the LM and made a skillful splashdown very near their target.

Apollo 15 and 16

Astronauts of *Apollo 15* and *Apollo 16* were able to travel farther on the Moon thanks to a lunar rover. From both missions, the astronauts brought back rocks. The crew of *Apollo 15* also launched a small satellite around the Moon to study its gravity, the Sun, and Earth's magnetic field. *Apollo 16*'s astronauts set up an observatory on the Moon.

Apollo 17

Eugene Cernan, Ronald Evans, and Harrison Schmitt flew the last lunar mission. *Apollo 17* lasted twelve days, and Cernan and Schmitt spent twenty-two hours outside the LM. In the command module, Evans did mapping work, took measurements to explore the inside of the Moon, and made temperature studies. The LM crew set up very sophisticated experiments, including new ones on lunar gravity. They collected a record amount of samples—over 240 pounds (110 kg) of rocks.

James Irwin, pilot of the lunar module on *Apollo 15*, loads his lunar rover with scientific equipment. The electrical vehicle chugged along at 9 miles (14 km) per hour.

After Apollo

U.S. astronaut Donald Slayton (right) and Soviet cosmonaut Aleksey Leonov (left), the first man to walk in space, together during the joint Apollo-Soyuz Test Project in 1975. The project involved docking procedures in space, something that became much more common after Apollo.

Cooperation in Space

In the 1970s, space competition turned into space cooperation. After *Apollo 8* and *9* had shown that Americans were very close to landing on the Moon, the Soviets had dropped their efforts to prepare a manned Moon mission. They still flew some missions, however, and by 1971 had launched *Salyut 1,* the first space station to be placed in Earth's orbit. About this time, President Richard Nixon began a new policy of peaceful cooperation with the Soviet Union. This policy eased Cold War tensions and led to the first joint space mission between the Soviet Union and United States.

The two countries had to overcome many challenges to carry out the mission. Some challenges were political. The Soviets did not normally allow reporters at their launches and had to adapt to having American and European journalists around. Some problems were cultural—the astronauts and cosmonauts required training to learn each other's languages.

Coordination

In addition, there were technical issues to consider. The two spacecraft had different docking mechanisms, and the chemical makeup and the pressure of the air inside the two cabins was different. That meant that going from one craft to the other could make the voyagers ill. Engineers had to design a docking module with ends made to fit each spaceship. The module's atmosphere could slowly be changed from that of one craft to that of the other, so the astronauts' and cosmonauts' bodies could adapt when moving between ships. Engineers also had to coordinate mission control, navigation of the joined craft, and many other aspects of the flight.

A Meeting in Space

The two space programs needed three years to prepare for the mission. But on July 17, 1975, history was made. A U.S. Apollo spacecraft and the Soviet *Soyuz 19* docked in space, and their crews met each other with a historic handshake. Once they were in orbit together, the two crews practiced different docking maneuvers, carried out experiments, ate together, and exchanged gifts.

The First U.S. Space Station

Meanwhile, NASA was working on a space station of its own, called *Skylab*. Launched in May 1973, it had enough oxygen, water, and food for crews to stay for several weeks at a time.

Skylab was a very successful scientific station. Crews carried out medical studies on humans and biological studies on mice, fish, and spiders. They studied Earth's water and other resources and took photographs of the Sun. They also

Hope for the Future
"How this new era will go depends on the determination, commitment, and faith of the people of both our countries and the world."

Tom Stafford,
U.S. commander
of Apollo-Soyuz

Skylab was launched on May 14, 1973. It was home to several crews and was used as a laboratory for many kinds of experiments over the following eight months.

35

manufactured new metals and used telescopes to capture images not available from Earth.

Skylab completed its planned eight months of service when the last of the its three missions ended in February 1974. The space station was expected to remain in orbit for eight to ten years, but its orbit began to deteriorate in 1977. On July 11, 1979, *Skylab* fell back to Earth. Pieces of the space station were scattered in the Indian Ocean and remote parts of western Australia.

At Home on *Skylab*

Three crews traveled to *Skylab*, where life was much more comfortable than on Apollo missions. There was a lot more room—the station was about as large as a three-bedroom house. Food was frozen or canned, and the astro-

nauts had ovens and hot plates for cooking. Astronauts could wear ordinary clothes inside the station—pressure suits were only needed for spacewalks and travel to and from Earth.

Crews had sleeping bags that hung on the walls and a special shower, toilet, and sink. They could use a stationary bike to exercise so that their muscles would not get weak from lack of use. During the last mission, astronauts Gerald Carr, Edward Gibson, and William Pogue stayed on *Skylab* for eighty-four days.

Two *Skylab* crew members demonstrate the fun of weightlessness.

Space shuttles are launched with two booster rockets (one is visible on the right) and a huge tank of fuel (the red tank in the middle), all of which drop back to Earth once the Shuttle is in space. The Shuttle lands like an airplane on its return.

The Space Shuttle

Starting in 1981, NASA's main vehicle for space travel became the Space Shuttle. The Shuttle is attached to launcher rockets for take-off and is flown back to Earth like a glider, making a landing on a runway. The front of the craft has the flight deck on top and the astronauts' quarters below. As many as nine people can live on board the Space Shuttle.

The large, middle section of the Shuttle is its cargo bay. Huge doors open from above, giving the crew easy access to space. This area can carry **payloads** such as several satellites or an entire laboratory. The cargo bay has a giant robotic arm with a "hand" at the end that astronauts can use to grab and move the payload. The back of the Shuttle has the steering equipment and engines used to power its movement in space.

The Missions

Space Shuttle missions are varied. Crews have conducted experiments in biology, astronomy, engineering, and medicine. One crew launched the powerful Hubble Space Telescope. Others have sent probes toward other planets or captured, repaired, and relaunched satellites. Mission tasks are carried out for the U.S. government and for scientists, businesses, and other countries around the world.

The first Space Shuttle, *Columbia*, was launched April 12, 1981, and returned to Earth two days later. Pilot John Young declared the new craft "the world's greatest flying machine." By 2002, NASA had three shuttles in service and flew several missions a year.

Shuttle Astronauts

Three types of astronauts serve on the Space Shuttle. Pilots, most of whom have military backgrounds, fly and navigate the spacecraft. Mission specialists are scientists responsible for the payload, and they make sure the mission's main tasks gets done. They use special equipment, such as robotic arms or manned maneuvering units (MMUs). MMUs are battery-operated backpacks that allow astronauts to move around in space without being attached to the spacecraft. Payload specialists are generally scientists who carry out experiments assigned to a particular mission.

Sally K. Ride (born 1951)

Sally Ride was the first American female astronaut. With a doctorate in physics from Stanford University, she was selected as a mission specialist for the shuttle program in 1978. Ride attracted a great deal of media attention when named to the crew of the seventh Space Shuttle mission in 1983. Although she was chosen for her ability with the robotic arm, reporters asked Ride silly questions, such as whether she would take lipstick or perfume to space. After her return, she had to fend off Hollywood agents and reporters who wanted her story. Ride flew another mission in 1984 and served on the commission that investigated the *Challenger* accident. She later wrote NASA's proposal for building a base on the Moon.

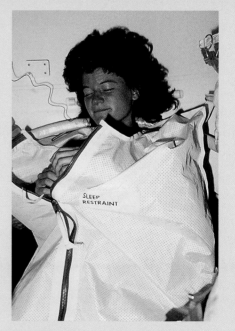

Dr. Ride at her sleep station on a Space Shuttle mission.

The Challenger Disaster

On January 28, 1986, the shuttle *Challenger* exploded seventy-three seconds after taking off from Cape Canaveral. At the time, it was the worst space disaster in history, and all seven crew members died. Later, the commission investigating the accident found that the shuttle had a series of structural problems. Worse, engineers had warned management about these problems, but the managers had ignored their warnings. The shuttle program was canceled for more than two years while parts of the craft were redesigned and new safety measures put in place.

Columbia

On February 1, 2003, there was another tragic accident. *Columbia*, which had been in service since 1981, was returning from a scientific mission with seven astronauts on board. About 38 miles (61 km) above the Earth's surface, the shuttle broke into pieces

Above, as *Challenger* explodes after liftoff in 1986, a launch rocket from the Shuttle heads up and away from the blast. Left, the crew of *Columbia* heads for the launch pad in January 2003. All the crew members died when their spacecraft broke up on its return to Earth.

The International Space Station

Starting in the late 1990s, many Shuttle crews played a part in building a new space station. The International Space Station (ISS) is a joint project of the United States, Russia, Canada, Japan, and the European Space Agency (which includes most countries of western Europe).

The ISS is made up of different modules joined together. Astronauts flying on Space Shuttle or Soyuz spacecraft bring the pieces and connect them. A Russian service module serves as the control center of the station and provides living space for the crew. The United States has added a large laboratory and solar panels that convert the Sun's energy into power to run the station. Canada has contributed a huge robotic arm, larger and more advanced than the one in the Space Shuttles. It can move heavy payloads around the outside of the station and help spacecraft to dock. The European Space Agency and Japan are working on additional laboratories. When it is complete, the ISS will be about 360 feet long (110 m) long.

In this picture of the International Space Station, you can see the Russian service module (with red writing), the U.S. solar panels (the flat brown panels top, left, and right), and the Canadian robotic arm (top right).

The powerful Hubble Space Telescope allows us to see far into space. These two galaxies, captured by Hubble in April 2002, are named "the Mice" because of their long tails of gas and stars. They are 300 million light years away from Earth.

Living at the ISS

Astronauts from the various participating countries have been living at the ISS since November 2000. Crews stay at the station for about five months before a new crew arrives to replace them. They conduct experiments in biology, space medicine, physics, and other fields. A "lifeboat"—an extra Soyuz spacecraft—is docked at the station in case the crew has to leave in an emergency.

Looking into Space

The Hubble Space Telescope is just one example of how space exploration today carries out important scientific research. Launched from the Space Shuttle in 1990, the huge telescope orbits Earth. Because it moves outside Earth's atmosphere, scientists get a much clearer view of the Universe than ever before and can see much farther into it.

When the Hubble Space Telescope was first deployed, scientists found that its mirror had a flaw. This problem blurred the images it sent back to Earth. Three years later, Shuttle astronauts returned with new parts and fixed it, and the Hubble immediately began to prove its worth. Among its early discoveries were forty billion new galaxies. A **black hole** was seen for the first time, proving the existence of these astronomical objects, which until then had only existed in theory. The discoveries have continued ever since.

Conclusion

This Landsat image shows most of Detroit and part of Lake Erie. Landsat images are taken from satellites and relayed to Earth. They help identify land features and population patterns, among other things.

Was It Worth the Money?

From the beginning of the space program, many people, including some senators and congressmen, felt that money spent on space exploration was wasted. They believed that the government should use its resources to tackle more pressing national problems. In fact, by 1968, Congress had reduced NASA's budget and by the early 1970's had cut funding for the Apollo program entirely.

While the money could have been used for other important purposes, the space program has produced many benefits. Today, satellites are used to track the weather, see how crops are growing, make more accurate maps, give directions to ships' pilots, help manage resources and control pollution, and protect the nation. Pure science is farther along thanks to the opportunity to study Moon rocks, the findings of the Hubble telescope, and the many experiments carried out by astronauts.

Advances in Technology

Many practical, everyday products have been created from the technology originally developed for space. For example, people with diabetes can now get the insulin they need through a small pump they wear on their belt, a method that draws from techniques used in the space program. The water filters developed for spacecraft have been adapted to remove lead and bacteria from drinking water at home. Powerful, fast computers are now common because the space program spurred research and development of computers. Even something as common as the sneaker is a better product than it was because shoe designers adapted advances made for the astronauts.

A New View of Earth

"To see the Earth as it truly is, small and blue and beautiful in that eternal silence where it floats, is to see ourselves as riders on the Earth together, brothers on that bright loveliness in the eternal cold— brothers who know now that they are truly brothers."

Archibald MacLeish, poet, playwright, Pulitzer prizewinner, and Librarian of Congress, 1968

The Legacy of the Moon Landing

The space program reflects two powerful human urges—curiosity about the Universe and a desire to stretch limits. The journeys to the Moon by the astronauts of *Apollo 11* and other missions have had a deep impact. Many people have seen the photographs taken of Earth from space, and those photos have profoundly changed the way they view the planet Earth and the life on that planet. Seeing their watery planet, floating like a blue marble in the vast darkness of space, has shown them how small and fragile the planet really is. This knowledge and perspective has convinced many people of the need to protect the world and all living things.

Time Line

1957 ■ October 4: Soviet Union launches *Sputnik*, first satellite in space.

1958 ■ January 31: United States launches *Explorer*, first U.S. satellite.

1959 ■ September 14: Soviet satellite *Luna 2* becomes first spacecraft to reach the Moon.

1961 ■ April 12: Soviet cosmonaut Yuri Gagarin becomes first human in space.
May 15: Alan Shepard becomes first American in space.
May 25: President John F. Kennedy sets goal of putting a person on the Moon.

1962 ■ February 20: John Glenn becomes first American to orbit Earth.

1965 ■ March 18: Cosmonaut Aleksey Leonov becomes first person to "walk" in space.
June 3: Edward White becomes first American to "walk" in space.

1967 ■ January 27: White, Gus Grissom, and Roger Chaffee die in *Apollo 1* fire.

1968 ■ December 24: *Apollo 8* astronauts become first to reach and orbit the Moon.

1969 ■ July 16: *Apollo 11* lifts off from Florida and heads toward the Moon.
July 19: *Apollo 11* reaches lunar orbit.
July 20: Neil Armstrong and Buzz Aldrin land and walk on the Moon.
July 21: *Eagle* leaves Moon and docks with *Columbia*.
July 24: *Apollo 11* splashes down in Pacific Ocean.

1971 ■ April 19: Soviets launch *Salyut 1,* first space station placed in Earth's orbit.

1972 ■ December 7–19: *Apollo 17,* last Apollo mission to land on the Moon.

1973 ■ May 14: U.S. launches *Skylab* into orbit.

1975 ■ July 17: Apollo spacecraft meets Soviet *Soyuz 19* in first international space docking.

1979 ■ July 11: *Skylab* falls to Earth.

1981 ■ April 12–14: *Columbia* completes first launch, orbit, and landing of a Space Shuttle.

1986 ■ January 28: Shuttle *Challenger* explodes shortly after launch.

1998 ■ December 6: First two pieces of International Space Station are joined together.

2000 ■ November 2: William Shepherd, Yuri Gidzenko, and Sergei Krikalev become first permanent crew stationed on International Space Station.

2003 ■ February 1: Shuttle *Columbia* disintegrates on return to Earth from a scientific mission.

Glossary

atmosphere: layer of gases and water vapor around Earth that provides living things with oxygen, traps warmth and moisture, and protects Earth from the damaging rays of the Sun.

black hole: small object, maybe a collapsed star, that has a very powerful gravitational field that pulls other objects into it.

command module (CM): the section of the lunar spacecraft that carried astronauts from Earth to the Moon and back. In *Apollo 11,* it was named *Columbia.*

cosmonaut: term used in the Soviet Union, and now Russia, for an astronaut.

dock: join two spacecraft together so astronauts can move from one to the other.

gravity: magnetic pull of Earth.

lunar: having to do with the Moon.

lunar module (LM): section of the lunar spacecraft that astronauts used to travel between the CM and the Moon's surface. It had a descent stage and an ascent stage, which could separate. In *Apollo 11,* the LM was named the *Eagle.*

navigation: use of scientific instruments and star positions to plot a course for a ship, plane, or spacecraft.

orbit: circle around a larger object.

payload: cargo carried on a Space Shuttle mission; doing something with the payload is typically the main object of a shuttle mission.

perspective: viewpoint or way of looking at something.

probe: unmanned spacecraft sent from Earth to another place in the Solar System that uses instruments to send back information to Earth.

quarantine: separation of a person or people from others in case they are carrying germs that cause disease.

rendezvous: move and steer spacecraft near each other so they can dock.

satellite: object that orbits some other object in the Universe. The Moon is a satellite of Earth, and many manmade satellites also orbit Earth.

sensor: device that registers something in its environment, such as heat or light, and sends a signal about its reading.

service module: part of the lunar spacecraft that carried equipment, supplies, and the rocket that propelled the CM back to Earth from the Moon.

slide rule: specially marked ruler with a sliding bar, used for complex calculations before electronic calculators were invented.

solder: join metal pieces together using molten metal.

Soviet Union: federation of communist nations in eastern Europe and Asia, including Russia, that has now disbanded.

technology: knowledge, ability, and tools that improve ways of doing practical things.

Further Information

Books

Dickson, Paul. *Sputnik: The Shock of the Century.* New York: Walker, 2001.

Mitton, Jacqueline, and Simon Mitton. *The Scholastic Encyclopedia of Space.* Scholastic, 1999.

Reichardt, Tony, editor. *Space Shuttle: The First Twenty Years— The Astronauts' Experiences in Their Own Words.* Dorling Kindersley, 2002.

Schefter, James L. *The Race: The Complete Story of How America Beat Russia to the Moon.* Anchor, 2000.

Sipiera, Diane M. *Project Gemini.* Children's Press, 1997.

Spangenburg, Ray. *Project Mercury.* Franklin Watts, 2000.

Spangenburg, Ray, Kit Moser, and Diane Moser. *The Hubble Space Telescope.* Franklin Watts, 2002.

Web Sites

history.nasa.gov/ap11ann/ NASA's *Apollo 11* thirtieth anniversary web site offers picture galleries, original documents, audio tapes, video clips, and everything else to do with *Apollo 11*.

spaceflight.nasa.gov NASA information about living in space, the International Space Station, and the Space Shuttle, as well as current news pages.

www.solarviews.com/eng/history.htm The history of space exploration is offered in reports of missions from the beginning of the space program to those planned for the future, including European and Asian missions as well as American ones.

Useful Addresses

National Aeronautics and Space Administration (NASA)
300 E Street, SW,
Washington, DC 20546
Telephone: (202) 358-0000

National Air and Space Museum Information Center
7th and Independence Avenue, SW,
Washington, DC 20560
Telephone: (202) 357-2700

Index

Page numbers in *italics* indicate maps and diagrams. Page numbers in **bold** indicate other illustrations.